Praise for *Transitory*

*The 'small and continuing dialogues in my own life' which Anne
Pia presents to us in this deeply felt and sensuous collection widen
out to span continents of feeling. They move from 'Asian bars on
Gothic sidestreets' to the 'tendernesses of tea' through landscapes
of loss and fulfilment, interrogating every aspect of lived moments
in graceful, supple and sharply observed poems. A real pleasure to
read.* AC CLARKE

*These poems are thought-provoking, insightful, grounded in
the senses, and very readable. Anne Pia's lively and engaging
personality comes through in all of them.* COLIN WILL

*These poems pull us into the worlds of others, taking us in so
wholly that we begin to recognise them as our own, tinged
with the same grief and love and longing. Unguarded and un-
afraid, her words give us permission to step outside of ourselves,
think as others might, and then see our own surroundings anew.*
MARJORIE LOTFI GILL

*The strength of these poems lies their personal voice – intimacy and
distance, immediacy and regret, the richness of life's experiences,
and its passing.* DONALD SMITH

I had the pleasure of just having a sight of a few of her poems.... I know that I'll read them again and again. The Spirit of Internationalism is with us still... DR DOLINA MACLENNAN

These are lovely life affirming poems. Wide-ranging in terms of subject, language and place, they are technically skilful, emotionally generous and a timely reminder that tenderness and love must prevail.
ANGUS PETER CAMPBELL

Transitory

ANNE PIA

Luath Press Limited

EDINBURGH

www.luath.co.uk

First published 2018

ISBN: 978-1-912147-37-3

The paper used in this book is recyclable. It is made
from low chlorine pulps produced in a low energy, low emission
manner from renewable forests.

Printed and bound by Bell & Bain Ltd., Glasgow.

Typeset in 11 point Sabon

For Camilla, Roberta and Sophie-Louise, with love.

Contents

Engagement and Dialogue: Selves and others

Authorship: The continual movement of self

Imprints: History, traditions and language

Acknowledgements

Special and loving thanks to Geraldine for joy, laughter and upbeat; also to the girls and Paul, Sheila and Monica. To Lindsay... you got me writing again after a thirty year gap! Thank you. To James Spence, thank you for the help with some of the Scots; and to my fellow poets – you know who you are – for rigorous and helpful feedback in the early stages of some of these poems. Grateful thanks to Jennie Renton for kindly editing and to Barrie Williams (barrie.williams.co.uk) for permission to use as the cover image his excellent photograph, *On the Edge,* the 2015 British Wildlife Photograph of the Year.

Preface

We live on the edge and in constant flux. Impermanence and randomness are what we have to work with throughout our lives. Like everything that lives and dies, we are in a continual state of change.

The opportunities and possibilities to be 'other' come through those we observe, encounter and engage or dialogue with in love. We also respond to the material world, to social and political issues and events. They impact on who we are and who we might become.

Sometimes new identities glimpsed and aspired to settle slowly and at other times we are radically remade. Our changing selves and lifestyles can also create change in those we are in dialogue with, and can alter the material world and the environment that we inhabit.

These poems represent some of the small and continuing dialogues in my own life.

Engagement and Dialogue

Social realities

We are in continual dialogue with the events and cultures of our time...

Monday Morning at King's Cross Tube Station

clacking tunnels
tiles' talk-back
zip lines and concrete
sound-sliced clean
the hunger games hour
a legion's eyes
whitened to milk
they storm barricades
briefcases bladed
their Jimmy Choos lasered,
pasties for gods
doughnuts for angels
extra heartbeats in cartons
a sexy sax
crooning
a blonde in tartan
whistling
rough sleepers ever rough.

The Redeemer left on the earlier train.

Monday morning,
King's Cross tube station.

The Bird's Eye: Remembering the Holocaust

One silent bird, colourless as the dry stones that bid him
and on which he sits,
watches over
a world without people,
of hollow buildings and chimneys now breathless.
It was here that the unnamed and the unsung
whispered their begging prayers
here where the steady drone of fear marked each gathering.
He always comes alone this bird,
to this place of reverent visitations,
where once upon a time
the ragged footfall of millions, ever watchful every one,
marked their passage
towards their last journey.
No fussing here about
hearty broths or Sabbath breads in the ghetto.
But it was here in times past, that a daily ritual,
of voiceless arrival and premonition played out,
and at the last, a realisation, a giving up,
a primeval recourse to Abraham,
thoughts of tender legacies, keepsakes,
all too present
at those inevitable endings,
without number and without warning.
Here, a simple procession signalling closure
on those fiendish games of hide and seek of decades
here in this dank place
where there is no song
    one familiar bird.

Lament for Jean McConville

(b.1934 Belfast, d.1972)

Cry, city cry, at the story of your Jean
at the orphaning of children;
not for Palestine or the Holocaust,
not for the mothers of Syria
or the children of Iraq,
but cry for your own generations and your lore
cry for each August, for your clockwork men
for the ghostly whistles and the beating drum
for the mascots and the trophies
the obscenities of your city walls
your whispering communities
and the ugliness of your broken streets.

Cry, politicians in your hollow assemblies,
cry, men of god in your pulpits and your confessionals
for yourselves and for yours
for the hatred in your cellars
the guns in your parlours
the balaclavas in your sideboards,
bullets in your kitchen drawer.

Cry, city cry for the bones of an innocent woman
for the earth that cherished her
and that finally gave her up.

New Testaments

and then there were
those wide-angled other men in heavy cotton
collarless shirts or Indian silk
coloured threads at their wrists
 fingertips of note;
men who on ordinary days
 in Asian bars on gothic side streets
Barcelona or Krakow
choose rice and pale beer
and who listen barefoot to Bartok
while lying low in Danish-styled utility
sleep in simple cots in light-filled spaces
court postmodern, Cadell fruit bowls
 leafy seductions even, of palms and bamboo.

Those gentle messiahs of the West
who in another life
in other places
slip soundlessly into makeshift
aftermath and dug-out
bringing us the salted cushions
of Afghan and Syrian women,
the red shadows
and trembling moons of children
who have already lived too long;
who have mapped earth's crust
learned the tides' legends
heard the murmuring of mountains
and the stars' ballads.

The contents of their pockets
of their canvas satchels
or slender iPads
can recover Tibet
with a well turned tune,
a portrait in sepia
or
just one beautiful word.

On the Eve of the Scottish Referendum 2014:
A People's View

There's them fer aye and them fer naw
an wer a done wi they 'debates'...
they articles in the posh papers
an the Facebook followers
wi time on ther hawnds.

Wer a sorted and wi ken wer brief
an ther's ony a fair few noo, fer changin.
But see if it's 'aye',
wel be gled tae see yon fat face o yours,
Maister Cameron,
fer aye, ye didnae expect it.
An yel be runnin aboot
wi yer constitutions an yer committees.
Yel be takin us seriously fer once
an wel teach ye tae respect us Scots
fer wer no as glaikit as ye a think
aye, an wer no sae hodden doon either
that we canny tell ye tae bugger off
a ye numpties in Westminster.

But see, wer no Norwegians or Swedish
an we canny gie free care tae the auld yuns
or pey fer gettin the mithers intae work –
an wer young fowk canny even get work,
they dinnae even want tae work, some o them.
An see too, wer no one country either... wer no,
they fowk i the Isles are aye moanin aboot
us fancy fowk in Edinburgh an Glescae...
an there's the Celts, an the Highlanders,

an the Lowlanders doon the Borders.
Salmond an his flunkies dinnae speak fer a them.
An ma question is, whae should vote onyway?
For there's an awfy lot o fowk livin here
whae dinnae ken us at a.

An if it's naw
there'll be a right fine change onyway
in wer fine land;
a land o bards, artists and an Enlightenment
that wusnae English,
yer seein a kind o democracy
never seen before in wer history
wer a in it... we canny wait tae speak
the bairns an the beggars
the taxi drivers an the wifies,
the jannies an the windae cleaners,
a o us,
risin like Cherlie wi his Jacobites.
Ye gormless gowks,
efter yon treacherous 'union'
efter ye and yer earse lickers 'cleared' wer land
pit us i the slums an the dockyerds
and the thrashins we got if we talked in wer ane tongue.

If it's naw, wer teachin ye Eton pansies
aboot a the people o these islands –
no just the Scots –
whit it is tae be a nation,
whit it is tae grab the power;
nae guillotines here, nae Arab spring neither,
jest the sovereignty o fine talk,
the will o the ordnary people
an the risin finally o the thistle.

The Queensferry Crossing August 2017:
A Celebration

Margaret, Queen o Scotland,
a pilgrim's boat fer pious purpose
ye gied us
when in Papist times
'twas tae Andrae's shrine
the world set its fute.
But efter creepy rantin Johnny an his kind
belchin blude frae yon eerie kirk in Dunedin's auld toun
wi they high-faloutin genteel,
Andrae's bones are there nae mair
lost in flames an fa'in stanes,
wha kens where?

But tho it be eight hunert years since
hark Maggie, hark,
whit graces saft an licht as air,
three maids in shimmerin robes
birlin, haund in haund, trailin bounty,
siller sheened, an aften gold,
haudin the shift o sun an cloud
midst fullsome skerts,
a fladden ower yon ficklie watter;
Scotland's flowrin spread.

There's nae dootin this proud-hartit nation's pert
nae dootin Enlightenment's star an the like o yon.
And on this very day,
anither declaratioun o alliances,
aye, yon proud brig o oors

contrarie tongues, erstwhile mixes
that wus for aye this nation's welcome.
In such wondrous feats frae humankind's
rer gifts an skill,
Scotland's brave proclamatioun
a novel Standard
in Chairlie's wake.

At the Day's Ending: Home

After the great homecoming of oceans
the fires of cloud forest and bush
the mammoth tumbling of timber
dry freeze of felled clouds,
the slowing buzzing of the twenty remaining bees
leaden river fish dulling,
the staccato humming of the lone bird,
there came a sudden settling of earth and sky,
and in the place left by a failed sun
they rearranged themselves on a new chequer board,
all the rules of engagement altered.

Engagement and Dialogue

Hidden and open selves

*Both our spoken and unspoken dialogues with those
most dear to us throughout our lives disrupt, uproot,
expose and continually rebuild who we are...*

Pierre… que je sois…

une pierre grise
et je promène mon doit sur sa surface
je bave.
Ronde, sèche, isolée cette pierre
elle garde sa solitude
même dans un tas de pierres
parce que elle est ronde, sèche, grise
et parce que elle est simple.

Toi, moi,
nous sommes complexes
et ne savons pas vivre dans la solitude.
Une pierre, a-t-elle besoin de pierre
mais pourtant j'ai besoin de toi?
Est-ce ma chaleur qui veut se propager,
mes mains qui doivent s'accrocher?
Ou est-ce que parce que je sens
que je ne sais pas vivre seule?
Je sens.
Sentirais-je si on ne m'avait jamais parlé
du mot sentiment?
Aurais-je besoin de toi?
Alors, videz-moi
séchez-moi
allongez-moi dans la terre
que je sois froide, seule, ronde, muette
que je ne réfléchisse plus
que j'apprenne à vivre.

Pebble

Lay me down in earth
drain me of all words
excise all feeling
dismantle me bone by bone
leave me out to dry in the winter wind
that I might be a pebble
round and dry
seeking nothing
no need to cling or feel warmth.
Or lay me on sand
where the tide will roll back my skin
cake me in rough salt
carve me small, simple
needing no more,
content to be solitary
whole without you.
Lay me down, lay me down
that I might live a different life.

Walking at Lake Louise, Banff National Park

You pirouette on glaciers
light of foot and heart
and all the while holding my gaze,
so as not to lose me, ever.
Black flies make a hungry assault on each of us;
we are invincible,
for now.
We warm at the dregs of a thin soup
twice.
On our way down, you sashay across a ridge, stop,
then return
to ease my fearful traverse;
I put my faith in your words, your deft hands
as you place each of my unwilling feet, one by one,
on a safe platform.
We eat an uncertain dinner
drink an unfamiliar white wine,
a brief first encounter with a camp girl in swirling skirts,
yielding rocks, high above, hold us close,
still green water, lofty pines and the entire galaxy,
all ours
for this one sweet moment.

Love Poem in Belfast

Some words are sweetheart small,
keeping other words company, helping some along
moulded and mellow... good natured sorts of words.
And again there are words which are as defining
as chiselled salt.

And there are the words which
bring surprise canvasses and
fine-boned sculpting to everyday phrases;
well placed and poised
they turn a sentence into a song
maybe even a country's heartbeat.

Say Guadalquivir
and waters will roll thick through darkest Spain
speak the words in Baudelaire's *Fleurs du Mal*
you will taste lava, smell sheep's milk,
croon your Gaelic ballads
you will tease life from flaccid green on island beaches,
you will make a kind of psalm.

And choosing 'I' or 'you' or 'we' is always a life decision
and the word 'they' maybe for me, a more natural choice.

But today, listen closely my daughters, my lover, my mother,
my grandmother with your rosary beads and my good friend,
listen
on this gentle pale spring morning
where steel arches high over a city dockland,
listen closely, for my word of choice is
you.

Afterbirth

This poem is about dreams coming true... the possibilities that
lie within the space between sleep and consciousness... knowing
and not knowing and where everything is possible.

in the small space
between waking and sleeping
a bird can still sing
stars still keep their promise
war-weary countries bring home their people
the twin towers still stand solid
a voice answers finally
my breath comes light again.

In that space of all right, of joy
beyond whispers
my mother unchanged by death returns,
sits close by
laughing her same old laugh
I am beautiful
and a small child
all purple and plum
looking only like herself
and smelling of olives and soft cheese,
runs unencumbered and unaware
of difference
with certainty, without fear in the machair.

She chases pigeons today
she will again tomorrow, and every tomorrow.
In this space her footfall is fluid, equal
and in uneven fields that tilt and lilt
among rough yellow grasses

my lovely daughter, a nursery songbook,
topples and rolls, is made whole
in a clear, happy light, unendingly shadowless;
hers a lifetime of freedoms
in this space, this silent cherishing
of neither end nor beginning.

Punch Bowl

Your thick glass walls
only got cloudier
and you threw old memories at me
of a fragrant punch with ripe fruits,
easygoing friends, uneasy kinship,
garden timelessness, take it as it comes,
when I carried you down the steps
of that New Town basement
that Saturday.
It was a warm otherworldly place
Old Curiosity Shop chaos
where the comfortably shabby forty-somethings
of the city
flexed fenders, balled door handles
stooped, scooped
chattering bolts, murmuring screws
for colourist apartments
astragal living in Fettes Row
and where come-and-get-me crystal
in showcase corsetry
flaunted its favours
and the solidly seated once black-haired woman
her brow fine and set
made my world ok
made it all normal
with a smile and the offer of thirty-five pounds
for the china, the cloisonné but not for you,
and as we walked lightly and in step back to the car
we vowed the rest of our years one to the other
and held our past happinesses close.

The Art of Walking Away

From your kitchen to your door
there are precisely twelve steps,
it takes less time from your bedroom,
though pace is a determining factor.

And each time is a new time.

I never mastered the latch on your gate,
not even that one last time
when I saw buttercups
at the cracked stone of your doorstep
fallen apples define the endless green
of the grass at your windows
and as you spoke your careful words,
a squirrel on your garden wall,
on his way home, I thought.

I heard songbirds colour your bathroom
spotted the packaging in your bin of your last ready meal
the earthy promise of garlic and basil's scent, long gone.
Your tobacco sofa, bought on a slow Sunday
where I should or would sit and sing to you sometimes
now gaping and still crumpled from yesterday.
In this now your space there are no guiding clocks
and we had abandoned music's suggestive commentary
on how we were or could be to each other
preferring neutral silence
or the happy-clappy presence of your television.

Your cupboards are a periodic table I know by touch;
from here I see that your white table candles

are still not entirely spent
the sellotape in your second drawer...
it will always quietly sit me out
the cheese in your fridge, that proud talisman,
always offering consolation or spice
should I need it
and in the unlikely event of you ever wanting it.

From your bedroom to your door there are eight steps
and from that other room of gentle light
of easier direction to and fro
there are only three.

Summer 2013

That was the summer
when the ground wasn't even
shifting unexpectedly... and without warning
sometimes holding me warm and stout, a firm encounter,
at other times we were at odds
with me having to seek level
and balance in unaccustomed spaces;
a spring summer...
when the August sky
light and blue
set a brisk pace
the cloud stream
always just out of reach
and the sun and rain took it in turns
to own my rough skin raw with the chase
with the yours and mine of it
the hollowing out
the masking and unmasking
the uncoupling of cup and saucer
and only the garden seat sat solid.
Then in the weeks after leaving
that house, a home turned pale,
the fresh arrival of morning winds
brought gleeful mouth music
mocking fragile certainty
and tossed my questions into the air;
and the watching Hebridean hills,
the unexpected new songs of strangers,
and friendship's cradling
finally brought glad, clear air
and a tin watering can painted yellow.

Counting Down

10
counting ten
the last bus is empty
she wants to stay
at least the lights are friendly
and she can talk to the driver

9
counting nine
a dark street
nothing can frighten her now
she watches the clouds
treads quietly
pinpoints the moon

8
counting eight
again a lost key
he answers the door
hello is awkward

7
counting seven
she hangs her coat on the staircase
both hover
green tea or red wine?
how easy is it to sit in her own sitting room?

6
counting six
who will she phone
texting her children
raking up friends
scripting upbeat

5
counting five
she fills crates
a life's journey writ in plastic,
frames and gloss finish
mustn't look
ignore the ghosts
a 'good morning'
the postman... dogwalkers... people laughing
laughing.

4
counting four
she marks up property pages
dreams of... of not dreaming
of no more questions

3
counting three
revising versions of self
when is tomorrow?
this is the one time
she must not listen to herself

2
counting two
'Why don't you stand on your own feet?'
her own feet can't hold all of her
can anyone?
She moves closer to the corners of her home
whispers her blue notes to its walls
gathers each room tenderly in the palm of her hand
where babies, teenagers and her mother slept once
and a suddenly ageing married woman lay awake
wanting more, wanting it all.

1
counting one
she considers the lives she didn't lead
loosens her grip...
stop.
Go now.

New Landscapes

you wear what's left of us on your face
turn of your head
slowed to a full stop
the generous landscape of your face
the melt of your mouth
all finally gone
to a new continent of intimacy;
and I pick up my bag
gather up my remains,
cross the well-worn path of your gaze
and at this taut, thinned threshold of an 'us'
my feet stick in the sludge of outside.

Haiku in Summer

Warm rain on the loch
Mute strangers sharing my space
I walk on wet logs.

           Giddy bike
           wild winds,
           gorse and bracken
           tack and pitch,
           Morar beach is
           bared.

Slow tread of dawn's light,
My cushion stills the day's breath,
I greet unseen birds.

Gaelic lilt and chant
Your face in careful shadow
Coy moon, trick or treat.

Summer in Knoydart,
in this house
of unrelenting space,
watchful
I
fear
me.

In the soft yellow
of island meadow
I breathe,
live in this strange place.

Rattling boats, stone's sheen,
Ruddy men hoist and gather
Proud bike standing still.

        Soundless, thin water,
        Among plates of light I
        pause,
        A ghost passes by.

Black flies on my face,
Warm hum of ordinary,
Hushed stones tipping red.

Legacy

What will you say of her when she is gone
your mother, friend, lover?

Will you think of cedar wood and coffee shops,
cool carved ironmongery,
spare lights from Sparta,
overblown exaggerations of cake
and the soft, seductive crusts of a well-thrown cheese
scone?

Or will you think of the spread of her smile
eclipsing uncertainty,
the crackle of her unexpected laughter,
like a tidal wave
washing her backwards
folding you and her in two?

Or will you remember her
in plum city concert halls perhaps,
hedged by oversized trouser legs
precise bobbed heads
and the heavy footfall of stout umbrellas,
where she, attired for no one but herself
and a random concert,
makes every symphony her own,
tumbles loudly
into the bold embrace
of musical coupling
and the titillation
of a well-turned triplet.

Will you think of a hallway
 love black-framed, proud and plated
 on a technicoloured tabletop
and floors flooded with sound.

But best to think of her tall,
standing on high,
darknesses of life's night spectres below her,
those fiery dragons of her history
mainly defeated;
her days lengthened,
her twilights strengthened
by the hopefulness of her journey
by the choice gatherings of a lifetime of loving
and by conquests
especially of herself.

Consider her often silent
in her time-tested valuing of you,
and strident in her
belief in you
and all that you have both been.

The Dream

on a night when suicide was no longer in question
running free and wild through soft stone
swimming butterfly style upriver
on floors of washed oak
flying up like a humming bird
I sang from castle ramparts
joined the quick stepping line-up
of heavenly sisters of charity
knelt in the chapel of repose
a cross at my throat.
I grasped Orion by his belt
clung on sloth-handed,
as the planet beat back the waters
fought to survive,
then beat out a slow air of retreat
on the drum of its afterlife.

Benedetto sia 'l giorno, et 'l mese, et l'anno,
et la stagione, e 'l tempo, et l'ora, e 'l punto,
e 'l bel paese, e 'l loco ov'io fui giunto
da'duo begli occhi che legato m'hanno
                    (Petrarch, *Il Canzoniere*)

Love Songs

One: Daughters

Her Facebook voice sings deep in me
I still make her rice pudding.
The answers to my daughters' questions
long grown all,
are still the same:
yes I am your mummy
yes, I love you this much
yes, I love you to the sky and back again.

And yes, I will carry you.

Two: Lovers

Why don't you come and sit over here?
(I love you)

Can I get you a cup of tea?
(I will always love you)

Do you want to talk about it?
(You stop my heart)

I'll give you a call later
(I love every hair on your head)

How's life been?
(I love you over and over)

OK then! Just leave
(I am nothing without you)

I am going away for a bit
(I love you, why are we fighting?)

Can I do that for you?
(There's a crumb on your cheek)

Will you please stop moving about
(Coorie doon sweetheart)

Will we eat this at the table?
(Sunshine in your eyes)

Three: Friends

My friend let me warm you.
How long have you been sitting here?
Will we walk maybe?
Can you come now?
Speak your truth.

Four: Mother

That voice that still says 'never give up… stand still'
that phone call that says 'yes'
the small bird that took me down a Perthshire
mountain
one Sunday in snow
was and is my Mother.

Five: Love Sonnets

Loving

a Commedia of words

lone litanies

sand through your fingers

Petrarca's blessings

always finding the one

whose smell brings you home.

Fear Can't Find Me Now

seated on a verandah
somewhere in France
secure in raffia and balsa
evening misting quiet
I remember possibility
and all the blue skies are mine.
I taste snow from geese coursing home
feel the heron's beak
plucking me from the water
the jet stream washes me innocent.
I see the colour of thunder
from the tip of a dockland crane
deep in Buenos Aires,
hear island bluebells whisper
in a gathering of grasses
at the end of the season;
travel dawn's hush on rainforest monkeys,
lagoons and trailing boats,
the day's first breath;
and fear can't find me now
I rolled it up strand by strand
dismembered it slowly
interred each piece
in the solid walls of found joy
drowned it in laughter.

For I am as fresh as new cut stone
building a ladder to myself
finding a way back
a new kind of nesting.

'One Fine Day' (Puccini)

One day I will own a garden
filled only with the light of early morning,
occasionally the sky's slow mellowing
at the day's closing,
city lights beyond idylls
pixellating a Van Gogh blue;
and there will be nothing in between.

In a corner by the wall
there will be olive trees
too many for us to count,
fruiting warm and plenty
at your settling there;
a gathering of open-faced sunflowers
will smile their happy welcome.

And we will no longer have any need
for memory or future
dispersing them like wheat seed
in a scirocco windfall;
every hour of every clock
will be ours to turn
or still.

One day I will own a garden
filled only with coy revisions
and beginnings.

Engagement and Dialogue

Selves and others

In different places, through different languages and words, we are 'other'...

John Durkin

(b.1926, d.2014) 'an inspiring father and partner'

My last conversation with John was about Dante.
He had found *The Divine Comedy* late in his long life
and I wish I could remember
what he said.
And at Loch Morlich that morning
a hen and her ducklings
were suddenly at my feet,
my only company
which I was glad of.
They tumbled over the crumbs of my dry breakfast
and I let the memories of him come – the man I knew
the man imagined, the man present,
or not.
At any rate, the man there
and the man now gone.

A man of libraries, of letters and big laughter
of people, politicians, and Makars,
John, both raw and so fine;
a man of flourish, a man of celebration
and a man of fierce and tender truth
gone quickly with little fuss;
and with him his proud and humble story both,
of roots, dogma and the communion rail
of renaissance and the freedoms of a thinking mind.
Tomorrow finally came
the clock's final round
the cat's cradle, our playground games of childhoods
forgotten, then remembered, then vanished.

Dislocation

(Anish Kapoor, *Suck*; Jupiter Artland, West Lothian)

How can you stand so firm and sure
in a wavering world of whispers, the mouth music
of forest
seeking out the spaces
where all your momentum
is barred?

On the Isle of Harris

Tender is the colour
of the grey dawns that heal
of Vango adventures
and uncertain suns which manage a smile, just.
My thin sleeping bag slips and slides
your hug warms my skin
you are another life remembered in an instant.
Dazed and still unfocused
on this new day
I grasp not without effort
both the wanted and unwanted
swallow a first dry meal
amidst strangers, unchosen bedfellows
earthy scents
intimacies learned and unlearned.

We sip a slow dusk
the sweet, smoking hum of our evening campsite
unexpected pinking of rock pools
drawing us thermal-clad
from our scattered private shelters
which will stand squat and sturdy in tomorrow's squall
for today and for this night
It makes us briefly visible
one last time
as we gather Lowry-like and sea-facing
unlikely spectators at nature's wordless play.
The purple vestments of night then
close yet another of these my very own days
of Marmite delights
timeless shells and reliable stone.

And I consider Hebridean legend and song
track blue mosaics on white sand
remember Ithaca and Della Robbia.

On each of these days of understated
I nod to that deserted house
still windowless
to its myths and promise
we never kept you and I.

In this unclaimed expanse
of watery green and light and tall grasses
I can rest awhile.

In the Royal Infirmary of Edinburgh and Trinity Hospice, Blackpool

Polished rocks sit proud
topaz fear hollows its grave
spent landscapes glare back.
Buzzing fear crawls low,
spring's stench on a quarry's lair,
What can you see now?

Considering Bees

This summer
I want to think about bees
squat on a pane of warm concrete
or else neat in a buttercup,
or undertaking a sunflower
quivering hulks, blackberry ripe.
At other times, they hurry past,
bristling with impatience.
Or, the season hushed and slowing
in private places
and fat with eggs and sperm
they are the queens
of fresh summers.

Hungry Women

I like women who are hungry
who pace and track
always looking for summits
seeking out pinnacles
never in shadow
often silent,
and ride alone;

women who stride and strike
women who straddle
women who swear
women who sweat
women who deal
women who dump;

women who lay hands
on wounds you had forgotten
and women who heal
those you have yet to have;

women whose place is always at the front
who choose their ice cream
without being asked
take up the whole seat in a plane
without looking round
send back a wine that's too warm
or a red that's too thin
women who move but don't dance

women who seek sex
but are never on their backs
women who are comfortable with labour
on good terms with their uterus.

I like women who are women
who stand stout in earth
their lives in their bellies
reach for their babies and their dead,
women who are princes
women who are kings
and queens
women who make women.

At a Paris Window

Looking beyond her window box
far from the croque-madames, pearls and palaver
 arched dignity, spoiled pavements
of high-minded Paris,
she warms at a memory
pauses at the farthest edge of now,
her bones and skin
all sucked dry by urban
and smiles at another self
in fresher days...
among pink wetlands
where the sweet breath of lavender and promise
was on her face;
at reedy flamingos with outrageous beaks
dipping and tipping in awkward balance,
and at bulky horses flaring white.

At this ringside of ageing here, now,
a Paris hearth which is not home
her shy parish boy
eyes still keen, sits newspaper on his lap,
she, eyes truffle-soft, seeks out
freewheeling summers long past
their hide and seek in purple grasses,
and the ripe soil welcoming their hasty, uneven spread,
the scents of lovers pungent like curds from stout sheep;
and those honest gatherings
of grandmothers and godmothers
mothers and aunts,
reliable archangels of rites
gatekeepers to vats of lore and legend,

who put aside for a pious hour on Sundays
the daily bread, cured meats of futures
sticky ooze of fertility, of death and birth
scrubbed hardy linens
and talk a language
fruited with wisdom and hearsay.

At this going and coming of decades
what is and is no more
in their shuttering now
she and he
grasp at a single hen's egg, at salted butter
and the tendernesses of tea.

The Tuileries Garden, Paris

Your approach to that white painted chair
which had something of Giacometti about it
in a Paris garden without grass..
backend of arty
is a precise green with white,
mild and magnificent
as well as your words and your hair bow;
and as you order your nougat glacé
gold rimmed and salon seasoned
you taste your every word,
and together with your grandson or so I imagined,
you gather the soft fruit of your vowels
lightly tread the idioms of your native tongue
speak with measured rhythms
aged in the casks of birthright and Gallic precision
and then the sun
moves on.

Good Time Girls

Ladies who wear linen
speak no languages
except mystique, and the loose grammars of
mind, rose quartz and angels,
the boom and bluster of Wagner.
And often while drinking mint-leaf tea in aloof theatres in
Edinburgh or even Perth perhaps.
They own dogs that drool or furtive cats that seduce;
these silversmithed time-travellers,
have age in their hair, wear sunshine on their feet,
orgasm gently at yoga,
wander dizzy through Stockbridge in loose clothing,
or cycle helmetless with baskets of stoneground fare.
Italian delis are their *campaniles*, Traquair their Giotto,
jarred pestos their cornershop frescoes.
In sparkling glass spaces of cool London galleries and only
on her better days,
they make love to Kusama, are attracted by insanity,
walk with beaded women, delight at cornrows,
swim in Edinburgh Dalry and often pause to talk to
lollipop ladies.
Copiously scarved, in newly-soled Birkenstocks,
they sing a cappella, in community halls,
airily swaying
to earth chants.
They do not salsa, do not run marathons, write with
pencils, never drive a boat or eat steak.
And seated on cushions which may or may not be Kidston,
one by one, the good time girls leave the stage.

Authorship

The continual movement of self

Only uncertain and transitory footholds in our self-making journey...

Waiting for the Film

I wish I was a picturehouse girl,
all punk and patchwork
rough knit socks, a scant covering
for that tattoo,
your gift for a birthday I have now forgotten;
a kind of Celtic branding, your style.
My hair is gothic geometry.
My lips are Hollywood, my face speaks tearooms
I am geisha rather than Greek.
And we would talk intelligently, you and I,
if I was that girl,
about the rise of Latin America,
the red tents of Jacob.
And I would live in Portobello perhaps,
with cats, a herb garden, terracotta pots
fifties chic;
I would dress my ginger girl in charity shop dresses,
listen to *Woman's Hour*,
and seated on rattan sofas,
I would turn the pages of a glossy book,
intent on Annie Leibowitz or retro Miyake,
maybe re-read reliable Austen from a library close by.
I would holiday in Sweden
play the mouth organ, ride on buses in oversized astrakan,
I would be that girl in a quiet corner drinking ale,
simply waiting for the film to begin,
and once again, you are fascinated.

Mandolin Annie

can ye no haud me agane
an al coorie doon
frae they safe thighs o yours
wi the tang o earth
an yer fingers rootin aboot me
tae find a guid tune.
A'l be that close tae yer hert,
hear yer songs i the makin
aw wee that a am
al gie strength tae yer airm.

The Manuscript of Monte Cassino

A monumental bronze
front runner of a Roman legion perhaps
or the foot of great Cesar himself maybe
broods the artist's silence
at the steps of Edinburgh's RC Cathedral.
Maybe it is Ulysses' arrival in Ithaca?
In his final years
Paolozzi, his huge hands slowed,
his restless bulk finally
constructed
sculpted by a wheelchair,
but still the pilgrim
sought home,
and a last unbidden courtship.

Holy Isle, near Arran

The blank page
unblinking, stony and silent,
demands words.
I could try to paint those shredded landscapes
stilled today in my dampened window frame,
give voice to a reckless sea
the clear, clean wind in ringing counterpoint,
or gift an image of
two white ponies close, one to the other
young lovers on an untrodden beach,
a cormorant set in stone and sunlight
a seal in a harbour of Scotmid bags,
chippy chic and diesel.
Or better still
the soft footfall of mind
in a mild room of apples, whole new bread
the currency of knitted wool, stitches shared easily,
the magma of thick broth
and a blue cushion.

Melody in Minor Key

It's all in the key you see
and oh the chill blue of that particular one
catching us all unawares
no resting here that's clear
and that's why I will take it with me
no pictures, for their faces are written on my own
no lock of daughter's hair
for the strands of our days together will ever bind me.

No it's the sheet of music I mean
when I go
and I will go
notes flattened to ease my passage
tease me onwards
for I don't really belong here with them nor with you
I will pick up that same old tune to guide me
as I have over and over again
I will fill every one of my pockets with it
fade away again into something major
bold again
for a while anyway.

Timebound

No need to look into the mirror
to find yourself changed and old,
seek rather your daughter's face
for she is both the child of your time
and a monument to you;
to a future
beyond imagining
or days remaining.

See where years already
ripple skin that holds her laughter
and folds her worries into its slackening self,
where they trace her hands,
buff the contours of her jaw and chin
to gender neutral.

Her bones are the keep of your history
her belly a live archive of your selves.
She is the you you might have been
the self your mother never was
nor all the women of other times.
In her face a history confronts today.
In her speech and every day
those generations present themselves
command our attention.

And on this day that we both share
 her breath is fragrant.

Come to the River

Past the black deserts of Nordic places
of Iceland or Norway,
where furrowed waters, those hoarse voices still, of ancients
stamped forever on hardy stones,
drop foaming and heavy
from vast platforms, and meet their level kind
settling into sameness
then move as one
in weighty masses to seek the welcome gathering of oceans,
their kinfolk.

From melting mudflats where you must tread with care,
be watchful of boundaries,
in Pentecostal fashion,
steaming jets, loosened tongues, spurt randomly skywards
savage in their quest
for cool freedom.

Mighty seas of the Americas, Asia, Europe
drawn at the bidding call of moon and planet
arrive with rhythmic purpose
on stripped, green-fringed sands of wheat-coloured grains
beaches of brushed white
or else dank, slate seashores.
But homeless, they only linger,
their cadenced withdrawal pre-programmed,
heralding fresh, new claims elsewhere.

But you must come to the river;
see its rush to flee the hill
its jubilant breaking and breaching
of tree and banks,
its wild unfurling
its frantic limbering
its dizzy dancing
its reckless carousing.

It roars escape.

The Baudelaire Quartet
Four poems inspired by *Les Fleurs du Mal*

La Malabaraise

Malibar woman,
let me build a hammock
across the expanse of your hips
and I will idle there;
lay down feathers on your generous belly
and I will slumber deeply there.
Let me take each of your feet
to nurture and hold,
fledglings preparing to fly.
For safe-keeping
consign each of your treasure-filled hands
and I will teach them a new craft of loveplay.
Between the buttresses of your glorious thighs
I will scent the sweetness of pineapples
and the spice oils of your race.
Loosen your scarf one more time
and tamarind will infuse
my breathy kisses.
And no, I will not take you to stern France
where concrete and grey
will fade and reduce you
pavements and parks contain and drain you;
but rather my dark Malabaraise,

stay soft on your mat
in loose robes of muslin gather bounty
bejewelled by tropical sunshine and rainfall
the offerings of coconut trees
and solid men of the sea.

Bohémiens en Voyage

I

Then suddenly they came,
shadowing the walls of the Old City
like hired assassins or a scene from an opera,
our louche guides to liberation
or to an exorcism of the mind rather,
perverted
by the Herodian darkness
of thresholds painted
with the frail, fresh blood of innocents,
and to deliverance from our nightmares,
sisters and mothers run through and
left stiffening on the cold stakes of Kalashnikovs;
and as the strobe lighting of bombardment
created fiendish slideshows
of body parts and decomposition,
of builders blocks on industrial wasteland, once a
treasured citadel,
of the hollowed out caves of al-Nahhasin its
bathing wells now parched
where East and West made mankind's history,
against the satanic counterpoint
of shells and bullets, a Paganini concerto perhaps,
heads down, we tenderly gathered our sleeping babes
new hatched chicks still in their shell,
in stealth herded our gentle grandmothers,
loaded dull-eyed fathers
onto whatever with wheels

and promised blessed manna.
We left water taps rusted with stories of ancestors,
stone circles ringed with our bonds,
pots aged with laughter and what it is to be home,
while our children watched a fantasy undreamt of.
In files dumb with fear and weeping
we followed hope, salvation
and these unkent disciples towards
a star filled desert and
a new Messiah.

2

May your children sleep well in safe beds
oh brothers and sisters of the West
while kindly fairies shape their dreams
the witches of our young lie in the filth of your borders
famine at your gates,
and cold on rough mats for sleeping
they feast on the spells of men
and vampires inhabit the spirits of despots and soldiers;
the rich man's table is closely guarded, his own secure;
Babel's offspring, the science of many continents
has built your tower and your bridges for travellers,
but who now will nourish your people
in its cleansed incarceration?

Note: Paganini was widely believed to have an association with the
devil.

Le Revenant

The chill of brocade and satin, my lush coverings,
is sweet with the cold ash and scent of you
 the rot of pit and broken slab that mark
the home we chose for you;
your world and not yet mine.
A new nocturnal coupling for us
your whisper-like covering of me;
gossamer teasing solid bone and gristle
you slip whole into my space
a noiseless breaching
by the light of a cold moon;
your scattered kisses sting
like driving snow;
and like a snake uncoiled
your glacial tongue, a savage piercing
turns my melting to ice
and I am your willing prey.
Then when you, my unholy prize,
slide away into early daylight
I your fearful, dark beauty,
am pregnant with your presence,
quick with our untellable fable.

Delphine et Hippolyte

Look now Hippolyte,
my uncertain lover, flushed pale,
see the watchful moon, our sole confidante,
when deep within these earthen walls
finally unseen,
my kisses, no longer captive,
settled lightly... a storm of fireflies...
on your great warrior frame,
feathering the ebb and flow, the ready summits of you;
like melting caramel, though timid at first
you softened at my touch
and within your bower's full blossoming, in the end bidden,
I savoured sweet damsons and the tang of nutmeg
which call me back
for our spray and scatter made oceans of our bedchamber.
And now, great queen, like those enemy tribes before you,
you lie at my side, my beauty,
felled and unruly,
and on pillows heavy with the scented rainfall of a first spring,
your gaze is on vanquished girlhood.

A still, soundless air surrounds you, my Delphine,
I am caught trembling in the evenness of your breath
I spin in your breathlessness
in closeness we are wordless
and as you watch me from where you lie resting
before your silent solidity I am both empty space,
and a fig tree, ever fruiting,
its yield always ripe.

I am your angel, craving a slave's unholy capture
your wakeful warrior, seeking no other conquest but you.
We have drawn back the drapes on innocence
my first full roses of discovery have bloomed for you alone
and in this chamber together we are abundant and victorious
but the cruel eye of the moon you speak of is upon me,
stark and unblinking in the dreadful black of this night.
In the coming of daylight
I fear for us and my reckless, insatiable loving of you,
only a half, unsmiling light,
our shared delight one in the other,
precious,
unblessed
and forever unamed.

Imprints

History, traditions and language

We are born into a set of social practices, norms and expectations. We carry those imprints through life...

Viticuso, 1913 and 2005

In memory of my grandfather, a prisoner of war who drowned
on the *Arandora Star*, torpedoed in World War 2, and of my
grandmother, who loved Scotland.

At the golden gate of this sparse country
long emptied of its youth,
its finger games and hopscotch,
and where we sat, my daughters and I
eating a handspun meal,
sipping red wine from lemonade bottles,
visited family, long ago interred in marble,
started at a photo of a woman we had once met
smiling out from her tomb under the weight
of a *mezzogiorno* afternoon.
Where we saw an unclothed sun
dip its rim into those sweat sodden fields;
was it here that my grandfather ate his bread and sweet onions,
while resting his back at the *angelus* tolling?
Or here that he lay to capture the woman
who courted with tricks?
Here that she danced her *ballarella*,
hankie in hand for decency's sake?

And in leaving that dry, slow place,
and putting it back on the shelf
like an unfamiliar book,
we took down, for this one day,
an odyssey to read together, maybe
like the Katie Morag granny tales we once loved,
an accordeon took us by surprise,
breathing life into that street,
as if replacing sunlight.

And I see a clog-shod woman,
proud duchess that she was,
standing at the crossroads, child at her skirts,
spun cloth across her back and legacy in her pockets,
about to turn the corner of her life,
bound for a land that would call her Mary, a Leith street,
a new war not yet in the making,
cots for her children which smelt still of oranges
a hurdy gurdy, the salt and grit of a cream ice,
Italian delights and satin overalls,
white-gloved car rides to country hotels, for a two-week treat.
She leaves this land to the ghosts yet to come.

And today,
in the white sand of an untrafficked Hebridean island,
a lifeboat, lost 'Star' of Italy, at its journey's end,
here and not there.
It scattered its load like roses on the water,
their shaming call in the seas' tides.

Italian Odyssey

It is 1st July 1940.

He is breathing cargo
and still wearing the reek
of twenty-one days in a cell
he is a traveller again, peaceable and without baggage.
Or sin.
There had been a visitor, late in the night
 but was this a time for host or any sacrament?

Before him, in the late evening
a cruise ship, *Arandora Star*,
proud in her dock, her deck now laced with metal
a crowning with thorns.
Mother for all ages, taking to her belly
all seven hundred...
sellers of hams, sweeties and flowers,
her dance-room floor is soft with boys and men
the air stale with uncertainty.

Then at sometime around 7am,
a last fling of a passing German boat
 a torpedo, the spider's bite,
a *danse macabre* in full fatal swing,
the sliding slowing
he holds a brother close, a first in twenty years,
 'Jump! Jump!'!
But there had been no sea in Lazio.
He stands erect, overcoated, elegantly poised.

The stranger's arrival is swift.

The Music Lesson

In a room glazed with the wax and ways
of another earlier time,
a room of the fifties... all mustard and musty,
straw hats bobbing like sailboats on a warm sea
of girlishness;
in that room
in a house of secrets in torchlight
and greening loaves of uneaten bread,
she told them they couldn't sing,
and all the operas of a generation were silenced,
fine-spun cantatas unpenned
and rising choruses dumbed to chill
by her cold tones, her disinfected majors
the steely scales of a piano
and the neatness of her smile.

The Man Who Was My Father

The dark man whose voice I can't recall
who was my father
offered me a boiled egg
one Sunday morning when it wasn't sunny
and you had left for Mass
when the gas hob in our ration book scullery was still,
the pots, our story books of roots and rooting,
of Italy and immigration, not needed,
they held their breath
and the bread bin where you kept the few pounds
my father couldn't find, kept your secret.

I can't recall if it was the yolk or the white
that I couldn't eat or why
but I can recall a room the colour of fudge
but without its sweetness
a tenement window which kept out the light
stale grass of our shared green below
the daily drudge of a pulley
my oversized cot a barren place.

And for the first time that morning I tasted frozen
like the chill on your face at some later time
at the opening of a door somewhere behind me
the draught of air that blew fear into your eyes
uncertain into mine as you did up my buttons
put me to bed, kissed me goodnight
and I didn't feel safe
and I saw him behind you waiting
for you to turn round
for the fairy tale to finish.

I can still see him now after...
your tears, the police and people
standing on the pavement below
in standard gaberdine,
dance hall lights behind
the man who was my father.

Remembering the A68

How well I remember this way and this road we chose
for our night escapes,
our journeys south
the promise of Scotch Corner
 the smooth, easy tarmac finally of the M1
its warming lights adding glitz to your glamour
to your legs and your lipstick, to my fine cropped style,
my trophy from another life.
We abandoned our sleeping city,
leaving it to burrow for its dreams,
those prima donnas of cafe life...
the gruffness of Gaggia,
toils of an ice cream freezer,
the fragility of espresso.

Maybe in those giddy days in the dales
and our search for a good gin and tonic
we were hoping for Hollywood, life in a Rat Pack
and one of us would be Shirley MacLaine.

Could we have seen me now, then?
My life's years piled high and heavy
the flotsam and makeshift of my days
barely ten years behind the age when you probably did
finally find those answers
to the questions we spoke of in our last conversation
you were so hungry to hear
you knew then how to recognise endings.

How easily the daughter becomes the mother.

Maria Coletta: 1888–1964

Sometimes you sang to me
an old Italian song
from the potato fields and the crumbled stonework
of that time and that place
where your jug sat proud upon your head
as you walked;
and the dough was warming
by a fireside where spirit stories hung
and love was shy.

And it was a song from sunshine
on the soft ground of valleys,
embroidery and lacework,
from Sunday bells, a saint's shrine
the Septembers of children, chestnuts,
the masquerades of festival;
and maybe a chicken taken unaware
for the stone bench you called a table.

And when you sang there was the girl on your lips.
For you always had slim ankles.

Some other books published by **LUATH PRESS**

Language of My Choosing:
The candid life-memoir of an Italian Scot
Anne Pia
ISBN 9781910745915 HBK £14.99

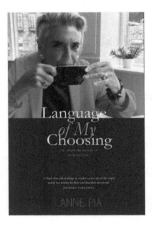

Where do I truly belong? This is the question Anne Pia continually asked of herself growing up in the Italian-Scots community of post-World War 2 Edinburgh.

This candid, vibrant memoir shares her struggle to bridge the gap between a traditional immigrant way of life and attaining her goal of becoming an independent-minded professional woman.

Through her journey beyond the expectations of family, she discovers how much relationships with other people enhance, inhibit and ultimately define self. Yet – like her relationship with her own mother – her 'belonging' in her Italian and Scottish heritages remains to this day unresolved and complex.

Shortlisted for the Saltire Society First Book Award 2017.

The language of the title is that of the author's self-realisation, as a professional, a mother and an artist. That language, born between different cultures, communities and religions, and between public and domestic life, emerges grateful, nurturing and affirmative.
MEG BATEMAN

Letters to My Mother and other mothers

Bashabi Fraser
ISBN 9781910745144 PBK £8.99

They forego promotion and pay packets.
They stay at home. They are night watchers
Who feed and rock and calm to sleep
They tie their precious gifts to their back
Or stagger in tired pride, pushing our future
They are the bravest soldiers – marching on.
– Mothers All

How does our relationship with our mothers shape the people we become? Does the experience of motherhood change us? Bashabi Fraser commemorates her mother and the conversations they would have together. Exploring themes of motherhood, empowerment, love and loss, the acclaimed poet draws on her Indian and British life experience, engaging with hard-hitting current issues such as climate change, war and the prevalence of violence against women worldwide.

A son questions his mother's love after she has learned about his violent deeds. The biblical Eve is shown as a liberator. A daughter of India demands justice from her society. Fraser's powerful, passionate poetry contemplates the experience of motherhood and celebrates the life of her own mother and of other mothers.

An Leabhar Liath/The Light Blue Book: 500 Years of Gaelic love and transgressive verse

Ed. Peter MacKay and Iain MacPherson
ISBN 9781910745472 HBK £20

The 2017 Saltire Research Book of the Year and winner of of the 2016 Donald Meek Award.

This collection, covering 500 years of transgressive Gaelic poetry with new English translations, breaks the mould for anthologies of Gaelic verse. It offers poems that are erotic, rude, seditious and transgressive; that deal with love, sex, the body, politics and violent passion; and that are by turns humorous, disturbing, shocking and enlightening. In scholarly introductions in Gaelic and English the editors give contexts for the creation, transmission and value of these poems, as historical documents, as joyous – or tragic – works of art, as products of a culture and counter-cultures that have survived centuries of neglect, suppression or threats of being 'burned by the hand of the common executioner'. After reading this book, you won't think of Gaelic culture in quite the same way ever again.

North End of Eden

Christine De Luca

ISBN 9781906817329 PBK £8.99

A polar projection changes foo we figure oot wir world. Shetland isna banished tae a box i da Moray Firt or left oot aa tagidder – ta scale up da rest – but centre stage.

Christine De Luca's poetry creates a sense of the beauty and spareness of Shetland, the contradictory space and smallness of the island; and a feeling for people. These poems explore concepts of identity, home and belonging, and of our connection with the land. Drawing inspiration from medicine, history and religious and pagan legends, from modern and ancient sources, De Luca awakens reader to the beauty of the language and the landscape of the most northern part of Britain; yet there is no sense of isolation. She explores the folktales and values home-grown in Shetland in terms of the wider world, from Russia to Canada.

In this collection Christine de Luca shows herself to be not only a heavyweight poet in her own right but also a trailblazer for the rest of us.
ELIZABETH RIMMER, NORTHWORDS
NOW

The Winter Book

Alan Riach

ISBN 9781910745939 PBK £8.99

The Winter Book begins on the ice and ends at the well at the world's end.

Dark castles of bad management and wasted resources are opposed by the forces of art, the virtues of openness, a gathering sense that borders are sometimes precious things that need to be protected, and that travelling across and beyond them is equally vital.

...full of big poems which encompass a range of experience, engaging with ideas, situations, places, and the why of it. Political anger is poured into strong, argumentative, emotionally engaging poems: no easy task.
GERRIE FELLOWS

The poems in The Winter Book *connect people, places and culture across geographies, nationally in Scotland and internationally in global, political contexts of loss and affi rmation, sorrow and anger, personal and public worlds, as memories fl ow into history.*
DOUGLAS GIFFORD

Fishing for Ghosts
Mike Harding
ISBN 9781910745854 PBK £9.99

Washing Hugh MacDiarmid's Socks
Magi Gibson
ISBN 9781910745472 HBK £20

In this new collection, Harding casts his poetic line to retrieve ghosts from the near and more distant past, his eyes and ears caught by fragments snagged in his visual and aural memory. A lifetime of listening, observing, thinking and reflecting produces poems that tell stories in his own voice; at times amused, bemused, angry or simply taken by the transient beauty of light in nature or a splash of colour in an urban environment.

Harding is a natural storyteller and, like all true storytellers, his direct language engages listener and reader alike in the recognition that their own poems may also be waiting to be retrieved from the seemingly random.

Some poems make you smile, others make you think, and all of them make you take notice.
AMAZON REVIEW

Mike looks behind the walls, gets into the words and music. These poems were written at the hearth, were written from the heart. They stay with me.
CHRISTY MOORE (on *Connemara Cantos*)

Magi Gibson, a prize-winning poet, explores what it is to be a fully engaged human in today's confusing world. These poems are insightful, joyful, witty, tender and yes, at times, rude. Two women in a punch-up in Glasgow's West End. A man stepping off a tenement roof on a snowy morning. An angry neighbour. A letter of solidarity to Sappho. Not to mention those dirty socks. Or that poem with the intriguing title, 'V****A'.

Tender and compassionate... Catches all the qualities of Gibson's best writing. Metaphorically juxtaposing the skeletons in her cupboard with the ghosts in her attic Gibson is a joy to read.
THE NATIONAL

Details of these and other books published by Luath Press can be found at:
www.luath.co.uk

Luath Press Limited

committed to publishing well written books worth reading

LUATH PRESS takes its name from Robert Burns, whose little collie Luath (*Gael.*, swift or nimble) tripped up Jean Armour at a wedding and gave him the chance to speak to the woman who was to be his wife and the abiding love of his life. Burns called one of the 'Twa Dogs' Luath after Cuchullin's hunting dog in Ossian's *Fingal*. Luath Press was established in 1981 in the heart of Burns country, and is now based a few steps up the road from Burns' first lodgings on Edinburgh's Royal Mile. Luath offers you distinctive writing with a hint of unexpected pleasures. Most bookshops in the UK, the US, Canada, Australia, New Zealand and parts of Europe, either carry our books in stock or can order them for you. To order direct from us, please send a £sterling cheque, postal order, international money order or your credit card details (number, address of cardholder and expiry date) to us at the address below. Please add post and packing as follows: UK – £1.00 per delivery address; overseas surface mail – £2.50 per delivery address; overseas airmail – £3.50 for the first book to each delivery address, plus £1.00 for each additional book by airmail to the same address. If your order is a gift, we will happily enclose your card or message at no extra charge.

Luath Press Limited
543/2 Castlehill
The Royal Mile
Edinburgh EH1 2ND
Scotland
Telephone: +44 (0)131 225 4326 (24 hours)
email: sales@luath. co.uk
Website: www. luath.co.uk